A GOLDEN THREAD

21 LESSONS CELEBRATING THE GOLDEN RULE
IN ALL TIMES, PLACES, AND RELIGIONS

Sunflower
education
*Exceptional Books for Teachers
and Parents*™

A Great Way to Teach the Most Important Rule of All!

The Golden Rule—"Do to others as you would have them do to you"—is expressed in virtually every world religion. From Ancient Egypt to Zoroastrianism, *A Golden Thread* explores this universal statement in nearly two dozen of the world's faiths. Students learn concepts necessary for them to excel in college and respond to thought-provoking questions, such as "Can observing the Golden Rule eliminate all harm?" and "What is the importance of scripture to religion?" A unique learning experience woven from many disciplines.

Grades 9-12 • 21 Activity Sheets • Complete Answer Key

Please feel free to photocopy the activity sheets in this book within reason. Sunflower Education grants teachers permission to photocopy the activity sheets from this book for educational use. This permission is granted to individual teachers and not entire schools or school systems. For information or questions regarding permissions, please send an email to permissions@SunflowerEducation.net.

Visit **SunflowerEducation.Net** for more great books!

Editorial   Sunflower Education

Design   Blue Agave Studio

ISBN-13: 978-1-937166-13-7
ISBN-10: 1-937166-13-9
Copyright © 2012
Sunflower Education
All rights reserved.
Printed in the U.S.A.

CONTENTS

TO THE TEACHER

"Do to others as you would have them do to you."
—The Golden Rule

WHAT THIS BOOK IS ABOUT

A Golden Thread: 21 Lessons Celebrating the Golden Rule in all Times, Places, and Religions is a workbook for high-school age students designed to stimulate their thinking about ethics, morals, cultures, history, and religions in preparation for college level work.

A Golden Thread achieves this goal by focusing on the Golden Rule—"Do to others as you would have them do to you"—and how it is a fundamental belief of virtually every major religion.

WHAT STUDENTS GAIN FROM *A GOLDEN THREAD*

A Golden Thread was created to do more than to teach students the Golden Rule, or remind them of its importance. Students who complete the worksheets in this book will

- Develop a deeper knowledge of the Golden Rule. The Golden Rule is expressed differently in different religions. Some differences are subtle and some are pronounced. Exposure to these different phrasings of the Golden Rule in various sacred texts elicits in students a deeper understanding of the concept of reciprocity and what underlies it.

- Appreciate the universality of the Golden Rule. Every lesson is illustrated with a world map with the general geographic area where that particular version of the Golden Rule was developed. Taken together, these highlights cover virtually all the populated world.

- Appreciate the longevity of the Golden Rule. Every lesson is illustrated with a time line that highlights when that particular version of the Golden Rule was developed. Taken together, these highlights cover virtually all of human history.

- Understand important terminology. Every lesson introduces and defines in context an important religious term (e.g., *dualism, pantheon*). The 21 lessons, together, provide students with level-appropriate knowledge to speak intelligently about religious practices.

- Be better prepared for social sciences courses. Religions are studied in anthropology, history, sociology, psychology, and other courses. A basic familiarity with many religions prepares a student for these studies.

- Reflect on important issues. Insightful questions help students further delineate and evaluate their understanding of religion and ethics.

How This Book is Organized

Each lesson follows an easy-to-use format. Quotes introducing the religion's individual form of the Golden Rule are followed by an examination of a defining characteristic of that religion. Vocabulary terms and questions ensure student comprehension. A graphic representation of the time and location of each religion marks a good jumping off point to examine the interactions among religions. Answers to the questions can be found in the Answer Key.

How to Use this Book

A Golden Thread will easily augment any classroom or homeschool setting, either as a stand-alone text or to enhance lessons in social studies or other topics as you see fit. The very first lesson will familiarize anyone new to the Golden Rule. Afterwards, the lessons on individual religions can be used in the order that best suits your needs. Each is self-explanatory, freeing you to choose your students' path. The final lesson focuses students on applying what they have studied to their own thoughts, offering an opportunity for self-reflection and growth. Many teachers have found it useful to copy the first page of each lesson and use them as mini-posters or as the basis of a bulletin board display.

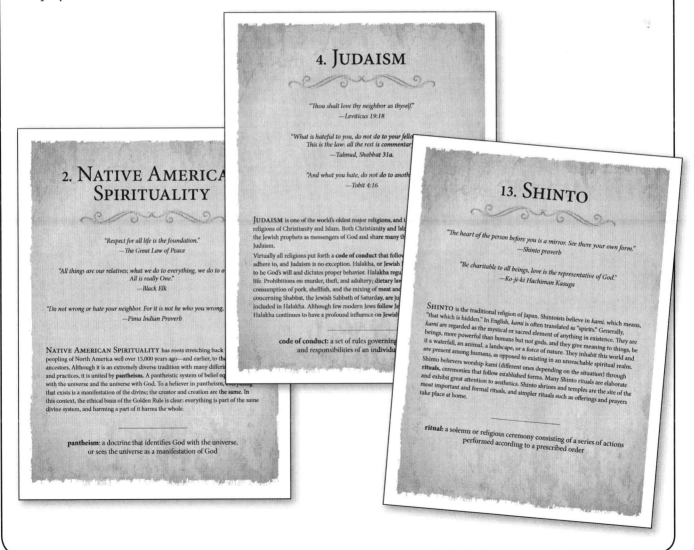

4. JUDAISM

"Thou shalt love thy neighbor as thyself."
—*Leviticus 19:18*

"What is hateful to you, do not do to your fello[w] This is the law: all the rest is commentar[y]"
—*Talmud, Shabbat 31a.*

"And what you hate, do not do to anoth[er]"
—*Tobit 4:16*

JUDAISM is one of the world's oldest major religions, and t[he] religions of Christianity and Islam. Both Christianity and Isla[m] the Jewish prophets as messengers of God and share many th[ings with] Judaism.

Virtually all religions put forth a **code of conduct** that follo[w] adhere to, and Judaism is no exception. Halakha, or Jewish [law] to be God's will and dictates proper behavior. Halakha regu[lates] life. Prohibitions on murder, theft, and adultery; dietary law[s] consumption of pork, shellfish, and the mixing of meat and [dairy;] concerning Shabbat, the Jewish Sabbath of Saturday, are ju[st a few] included in Halakha. Although few modern Jews follow Je[wish law] Halakha continues to have a profound influence on Jewish [life.]

code of conduct: a set of rules governing [the behavior] and responsibilities of an individu[al]

2. NATIVE AMERICA[N] SPIRITUALITY

"Respect for all life is the foundation."
—*The Great Law of Peace*

"All things are our relatives; what we do to everything, we do to o[urselves.] All is really One."
—*Black Elk*

"Do not wrong or hate your neighbor. For it is not he who you wrong, [but yourself.]"
—*Pima Indian Proverb*

NATIVE AMERICAN SPIRITUALITY has roots stretching back [to the] peopling of North America well over 15,000 years ago—and earlier, to th[eir] ancestors. Although it is an extremely diverse tradition with many differ[ing beliefs] and practices, it is united by **pantheism.** A pantheistic system of belief eq[uates] with the universe and the universe with God. To a believer in pantheism, [everything] that exists is a manifestation of the divine; the creator and creation are the same. In this context, the ethical basis of the Golden Rule is clear: everything is part of the same divine system, and harming a part of it harms the whole.

pantheism: a doctrine that identifies God with the universe, or sees the universe as a manifestation of God

13. SHINTO

"The heart of the person before you is a mirror. See there your own form."
—*Shinto proverb*

"Be charitable to all beings, love is the representative of God."
—*Ko-ji-ki Hachiman Kasuga*

SHINTO is the traditional religion of Japan. Shintoists believe in *kami*, which means, "that which is hidden." In English, *kami* is often translated as "spirits." Generally, *kami* are regarded as the mystical or sacred element of anything in existence. They are beings, more powerful than humans but not gods, and they give meaning to things, be it a waterfall, an animal, a landscape, or a force of nature. They inhabit this world and are present among humans, as opposed to existing in an unreachable spiritual realm. Shinto believers worship *kami* (different ones depending on the situation) through **rituals,** ceremonies that follow established forms. Many Shinto rituals are elaborate and exhibit great attention to aesthetics. Shinto shrines and temples are the site of the most important and formal rituals, and simpler rituals such as offerings and prayers take place at home.

ritual: a solemn or religious ceremony consisting of a series of actions performed according to a prescribed order

Glossary of Religious Terms
Discussed in this Book

ASCETICISM the practice of strict self-discipline and self-denial, usually for religious or spiritual reasons

CODE OF CONDUCT a set of rules governing proper behavior and responsibilities of an individual or group

DOCTRINE OF SALVATION a set of beliefs concerning deliverance from sin and its consequences

DUALISM the religious doctrine that the universe contains opposed powers of good and evil

FOUNDER originator or creator of a religion

HENOTHEISM the worship of one god without denying the existence of other gods.

MEDITATION engaging in mental exercise (as concentration on one's breathing or repetition of a mantra) for the purpose of reaching a heightened level of spiritual awareness

MONOTHEISM the doctrine or belief that there is only one true god

MYSTICISM the belief that direct knowledge of god, spiritual truth, or ultimate reality can be attained through subjective experience (as intuition or insight)

NEOPAGANISM a modern religious movement that seeks to incorporate beliefs or ritual practices from traditions from outside the main world religions, especially pre-Christian Europe and North America

NON-CREEDAL the property of lacking a set of beliefs

NONTHEISM the absence of belief in a deity

PANTHEISM a doctrine that identifies god with the universe, or sees the universe as a manifestation of god

POLYTHEISM the belief in or worship of more than one god

REINCARNATION the rebirth of a soul in a new body

RELIGION belief in and worship of one or more deities

RITUAL a solemn or religious ceremony consisting of a series of actions performed according to a prescribed order

SCRIPTURE a body of writings considered sacred or authoritative

SECULAR denoting attitudes, activities, or other things that have no religious or spiritual basis

SYNCRETISM the combination of different beliefs or practices; the amalgamation of different religions

Table of Religions
Discussed in this Book

Religion	Founded	Founder	Sacred Text(s)
Native American Spirituality	Various circa 15000 B.C.E., North and South America	many unknown	various
Ancient Egyptian Religion	Various circa 3000 B.C.E., Egypt	unknown	various
Judaism	circa 2000-1500 B.C.E., Israel	Abraham	*The Tanakh* (Hebrew Bible), *Talmud*
Hinduism	circa second and first millennium B.C.E., India	unknown	*The Vedas, Upanishads, Bhagavad Gita,* et al.
Zoroastrianism	circa 12th century B.C.E, Iran	Zoroaster	*The Avesta*
Confucianism	circa 550 B.C.E., China	Ch'iu K'ung (Confucius)	*Analects*
Jainism	circa 550 B.C.E., India	Mahavira	The teachings of Mahavira
Buddhism	circa 500 B.C.E, India	Siddhartha Gautama (Gautama Buddha)	The Pali Canon, Mahayana Sutras
Roman Pagan Religion	circa 550 B.C.E., Rome	various	various
Taoism	circa 300 B.C.E., China	Lao Tzu	*Tao Te Ching*
Christianity	circa 30 C.E., Israel	Jesus	The Bible
Shinto	Circa 500 C.E., Japan	unknown	Historical texts (the *Kojiki, Shohu Nihongi, Rikkokushi,* and *Jinno Shitoki*)
Islam	622 C.E., Saudi Arabia	Muhammed	*The Qur'an, The Hadith*
Sufism	622 C.E., Saudi Arabia	Muhammed	*The Qur'an, The Hadith*
Sikhism	1469 C.E., Punjab region	Guru Nanak	*Guru Granth Sahib*
Humanism	circa 1400 C.E., Italy	various	N/A
Baha'i	1852 C.E., Iran	Mirza Husayn-Ali (Baha'u'llah)	The writings of the Bab and Baha'u'llah
Wicca	circa 1950 C.E., England	various	The Wiccan Rede, et al.
Unitarian Universalism	1961 C.E., USA	various	any, all, or none

ANSWER KEY

1. UNDERSTANDING THE GOLDEN RULE

1. Answers will vary slightly. Rule of ethical conduct: provides guidance for proper or moral behavior; religious teaching: taught by virtually every religion; maxim: it is a short, pithy statement providing general guidance.

2. 1. a belief in a deity or deities or in some other greater power; 2. a belief in salvation; 3. the use of religious rituals; 4. the use of religious tales; 5. a code of conduct.

3. Answers will vary, but will allude to the universality of the human experience or the inherent advantages of reciprocity.

2. NATIVE AMERICAN SPIRITUALITY

1. Responses will vary, but should demonstrate an understanding that God and the universe are inextricably linked or are one in the same.

2. Answers will vary but should be well–reasoned. Could include discussion of concern for environmental issues, preservation of life, a non–anthropocentric (human–centered) view of the world, etc.

3. Responses will vary. One main difference, especially regarding the first two quotes, is that the Golden Rule is applied to all life instead of being limited to humanity. Only Jainism shares this aspect.

3. ANCIENT EGYPTIAN RELIGION

1. Answers will vary but should demonstrate an ability to think critically. The form of the Egyptian Golden Rule differs from most others in that it does not mandate consideration of the wishes and feelings of others.

2. Answers will vary, but should demonstrate critical thinking. Students may allude to the universality of inequality and the challenge that this presents in adhering to the Golden Rule.

3. Answers will vary, but should be supported with a logical argument.

4. JUDAISM

1. Answers will vary but should offer sufficient explanation for the stance taken.

2. Answers will vary and should be judged on the strength of their argumentation.

5. HINDUISM

1. Answers will vary but should demonstrate an understanding that karma is the sum of a soul's actions in this and previous lives and determines the state and status of reincarnation, and that reincarnation is the rebirth of a soul in a new body.

2. Answers will vary but should be well–reasoned. Could include discussion of observing the Golden Rule as a means for the soul to pursue perfection through gaining good karma.

6. ZOROASTRIANISM

1. Answers will vary. Could include discussion of universal vs. relative ethics or a refutation of good and evil having an effect on the Golden Rule.

2. Answers will vary slightly. They should note the positive nature of "Do to others…" as opposed to the negative nature of "Whatever is disagreeable…."

7. CONFUCIANISM

1. Answers will vary but should be well–reasoned. Could include discussion of China's top-down governmental structure, loyalty to family, respect and reverence for the elderly, the importance of "saving face", and hierarchical social structures.

2. Answers should affirm or negate the positive impact of the Golden Rule and provide justification, and demonstrate an ability to think critically.

8. Jainism

1. Answers will vary but should demonstrate an understanding of how the Golden Rule functions as an ethical principle.
2. To lie by not telling the whole truth or to mislead by leaving out crucial information.
3. Answers will vary, but should allude to the broader inclusion of all living things in the Golden Rule of Jainism.

9. Buddhism

1. Answers will vary but should demonstrate an understanding of nontheism. Might include discussion of commitment to personal spiritual growth vs. submission to divine will.
2. Answers will vary but should demonstrate an understanding that Buddhists do not worship a deity. Perhaps the lack of a deity increases the responsibility of people to live moral lives, in part by following the Golden Rule.

10. Roman Pagan Religion

1. Answers will vary but should exhibit an effort to think critically and weigh relative merits of ethical decisions.
2. Answers will vary but may include the ability to relate more easily to an imperfect god or the desire for a perfect example to strive towards. Reward thoughtful responses.

11. Taoism

1. Answers will vary but should demonstrate an effort to think critically about human needs and the human condition. Encourage thinking about the consequences of taking anything to excess.
2. Answers will vary but should be well–supported, and might include seeking harmony, order, and balance at the social level.

12. Christianity

1. A doctrine of salvation allows believers to rectify their transgressions and mistakes in life, and provides a path to reward, such as eternal life.
2. Because it was stated by Jesus.
3. Answers may refer to the spread of Christianity through Christian Europe's expansion and other missionary activities.

13. Shinto

1. Responses will vary but should evaluate differences in beliefs concerning the interaction of the spiritual and the material realms.
2. Answers will vary but may include that rituals function as formalized worship and are a way for believers to participate in religion, can build community and cohesion among believers, and can be an active demonstration of beliefs.

14. Islam

1. Answers will vary but should be well-reasoned and reflect an understanding of monotheism.
2. Prophets serve as messengers of a deity, intermediaries between humanity and the divine, and illuminate the will of the deity.

15. Sufism

1. Answers will vary but should demonstrate an understanding of mysticism and its focus on direct experience.
2. Answers will vary but should be well–reasoned and evaluate mysticism's principles and its purpose, and attempt to place it in a broader context. Perhaps the feelings associated with mysticism are fundamental to the human or religious experience.

16. SIKHISM

1. Answers should demonstrate an understanding of the role of scripture in religion, particularly how it often, but not always, represents the will of a deity and forms the basis for theological development.

2. Answers will vary but should be well–reasoned and demonstrate knowledge of the structure and functioning of different religions. Religions that lack scriptures are often non-creedal or non-dogmatic (such as Unitarian Universalism) or are based on oral traditions.

3. Answers will vary. Reward thoughtful responses.

17. HUMANISM

1. Responses will vary but should be explained. Perhaps that the concept of reciprocity is rooted in the human experience.

2. Answers will vary but should be logical. May include religions influencing each other, the Golden Rule's simplicity, its usefulness as an ethical principle, or other similarities among religions.

18. BAHA'I

1. Syncretism is an amalgamation of different religions. Baha'i provides an example of syncretism because it combines beliefs and traditions from all of the major religions to form a distinct new religion.

2. Answers will vary but should demonstrate an effort to think critically about ethics. Reward thoughtful responses.

19. WICCA

1. Answers will vary but should be supported. The Rede functions the same as the Golden Rule, but lacks the reciprocal formulation of most versions.

2. Answers will vary but should be well–reasoned. Answers might include comments on the nexus between humanity and nature,

the role of natural cycles in human life, or the universality of many cycles.

3. Responses will vary but should be logically sound. Might include discussion of alienation from nature, industrialization, the structured and rule-oriented nature of modern life, or other pressures.

20. UNITARIAN UNIVERSALISM

1. Answers should demonstrate an understanding of *creed*. Creeds serve to unify beliefs and believers, and sometimes are a formal statement at the heart of a religion.

2. Answers should be well–supported by logical reasoning. Criticisms of the Golden Rule include: one action can have multiple consequences, some beneficial and some harmful, for multiple people or groups; people have differing moral norms and different expectations of how they ought to be treated; and that it ensures consistency more than morality. A response in the affirmative must provide an argument for the universal validity of the Golden Rule. Reward thoughtful responses.

21. FOLLOWING THE GOLDEN RULE

1. Answers will vary. Reward thoughtful responses.

2. Answers will vary, but be supported logically. Reward thoughtful responses.

3. Answers will vary. Students should display an understanding of reciprocity and express how their expectations were met or not.

4. Answers will vary. Students should demonstrate an understanding of reciprocity (positive or negative) and note the commonality of this concept throughout the world's religions.

5. Students may circle the entire map and indicate the entire length of the time line.

"We have committed the Golden Rule to memory; let us now commit it to life."

—Edwin Markham (1852-1940), American Poet

1. Understanding the Golden Rule

Golden Rule (noun) a rule of ethical conduct, religious teaching, and maxim that states that one should behave toward others as one would have others behave toward oneself; in the West it is commonly phrased "Do to others as you would have them do to you."

THE GOLDEN RULE is called "golden" because it is the highest and finest rule for living one's life.

Living in a country steeped in Christian tradition, most Americans know the Biblical version of the golden rule. One version is in the definition above. The other is of Jesus Christ saying, during the Sermon on the Mount, "So whatever you wish that men would do to you, do so to them."

Most Americans think of the Golden Rule as a Christian concept. And it is. But the Golden Rule is also a fundamental principle of virtually every other religion as well.

All societies have **religion.** The variety of religions today, and over the course of history, is mind-boggling. That's why finding a common element—the Golden Rule— is so rewarding.

Scholars have identified five elements that all religions share: a belief in a deity or deities or in some other greater power; a belief in salvation, or the idea that individuals can be saved; the use of religious rituals; the use of religious tales (parables, stories, legends, and so on); and, finally, a code of conduct, or rules for living.

Codes of conduct among the many religions include a variety of rules about behavior, including such things as proper dress, foodstuffs, performance of rites, and so on. Because of the stunning variety of religions, these rules for living vary dramatically. Yet, again, the Golden Rule appears consistently in virtually all religions' codes of conduct.

---

religion: belief in and worship of one or more deities

① How is the Golden Rule all of the following: a rule of ethical conduct, a religious teaching, and a maxim?

_____

_____

_____

② What are the five elements that all *religions* have in common? List them, and underline the one into which the Golden Rule falls.

_____

_____

_____

③ Why do you think the Golden Rule is a fundamental teaching of nearly every religion? Use additional pages if needed.

_____

_____

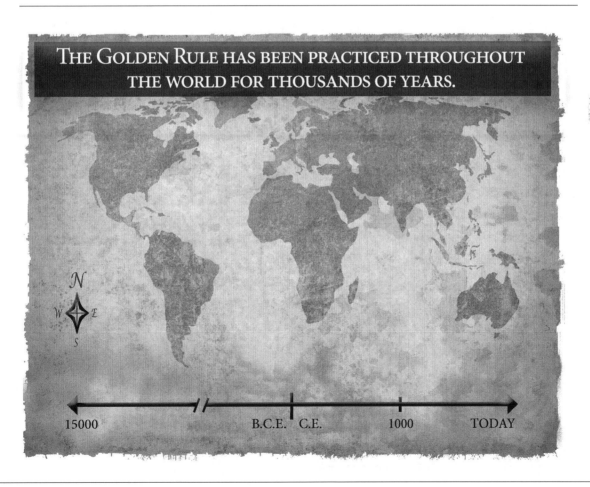

THE GOLDEN RULE HAS BEEN PRACTICED THROUGHOUT THE WORLD FOR THOUSANDS OF YEARS.

15000   B.C.E.   C.E.   1000   TODAY

2. NATIVE AMERICAN SPIRITUALITY

"Respect for all life is the foundation."
—The Great Law of Peace

*"All things are our relatives; what we do to everything, we do to ourselves.
All is really One."*
—Black Elk

"Do not wrong or hate your neighbor. For it is not he who you wrong, but yourself."
—Pima Indian Proverb

NATIVE AMERICAN SPIRITUALITY has roots stretching back to the first peopling of North America well over 15,000 years ago—and earlier, to their Asian ancestors. Although it is an extremely diverse tradition with many differing rituals and practices, it is united by **pantheism.** A pantheistic system of belief equates God with the universe and the universe with God. To a believer in pantheism, everything that exists is a manifestation of the divine; the creator and creation are the same. In this context, the ethical basis of the Golden Rule is clear: everything is part of the same divine system, and harming a part of it harms the whole.

---

pantheism: a doctrine that identifies God with the universe,
or sees the universe as a manifestation of God

① Explain *pantheism* in your own words.

_____

_____

_____

② How might pantheism influence a people's worldview?

_____

_____

_____

③ Does the Golden Rule of Native American spirituality seem to differ from one that you know? Explain.

_____

_____

_____

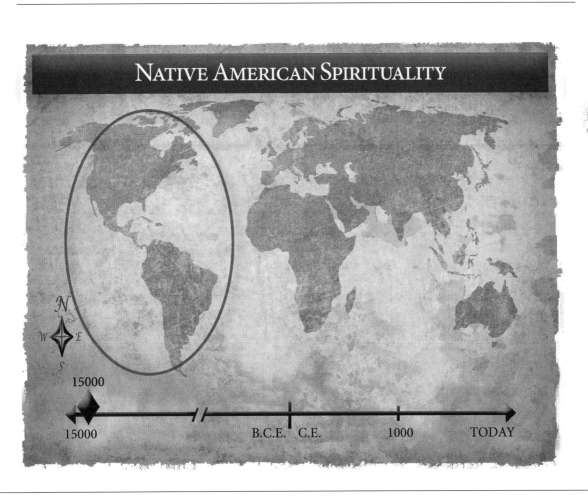

NATIVE AMERICAN SPIRITUALITY

3. Ancient Egyptian Religion

"Do for one who may do for you, that you may cause him thus to do."
—The Tale of the Eloquent Peasant

The ancient Egyptians believed in an immense pantheon, or group of deities. They sought to appease the gods and goddesses and win their favor through elaborate rituals and offerings. The rulers of ancient Egypt—the Pharaohs—were believed to have a divine presence and a special communion with the gods, so they ruled by divine right and had the ultimate responsibility to ensure the gods' favor.

Generally, scholars have categorized this ancient religion as a henotheistic system. **Henotheism** refers to a religious system in which followers worship primarily or solely one god while acknowledging other gods might or do exist. The ancient Egyptians fit this pattern, in that worship was usually directed primarily towards a single god. Exactly which god was focused on changed over time and place, and at times devotees of different gods competed to have their favored deity worshipped most widely. At all times, and places, however, a code of conduct that included a version of the Golden Rule was present.

---

henotheism: the worship of one god without denying the existence of other gods

① Evaluate this statement: the Golden Rule of the ancient Egyptian religion is rooted in self-interest rather than reciprocity.

_____

_____

② Ancient Egypt was a hierarchical society. How do you think the Golden Rule can exist in such an environment?

_____

_____

_____

③ Should _henotheism_ be regarded as a category of religion separate from polytheism, which is the worship of many gods? Why or why not?

_____

_____

_____

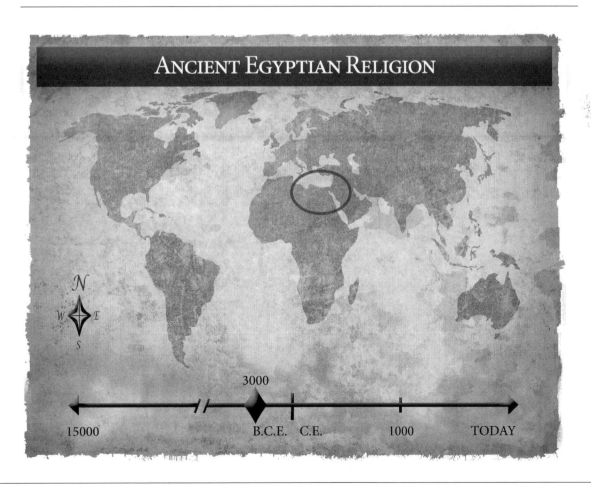

ANCIENT EGYPTIAN RELIGION

4. Judaism

"Thou shalt love thy neighbor as thyself."
—Leviticus 19:18

*"What is hateful to you, do not do to your fellow man.
This is the law: all the rest is commentary."*
—Talmud, Shabbat 31a.

"And what you hate, do not do to another."
—Tobit 4:16

JUDAISM is one of the world's oldest major religions, and the root of the later religions of Christianity and Islam. Both Christianity and Islam acknowledge all of the Jewish prophets as messengers of God and share many theological concepts with Judaism.

Virtually all religions put forth a **code of conduct** that followers are expected to adhere to, and Judaism is no exception. Halakha, or Jewish Law, is believed by Jews to be God's will and dictates proper behavior. Halakha regulates many aspects of life. Prohibitions on murder, theft, and adultery; dietary laws (kosher) banning the consumption of pork, shellfish, and the mixing of meat and dairy; and regulations concerning Shabbat, the Jewish Sabbath of Saturday, are just a few examples of laws included in Halakha. Although few modern Jews follow Jewish law to the letter, Halakha continues to have a profound influence on Jewish life.

---

code of conduct: a set of rules governing proper behavior
and responsibilities of an individual or group

① Do you think the Golden Rule is a sufficient guideline, or is a more detailed *code of conduct* necessary? Explain.

_____

_____

_____

_____

_____

② In your opinion, which of the following is more important: that a religion adapts to the needs of people in the modern world, or that a religion maintains its long-held customs and practices? Explain your reasoning.

_____

_____

_____

_____

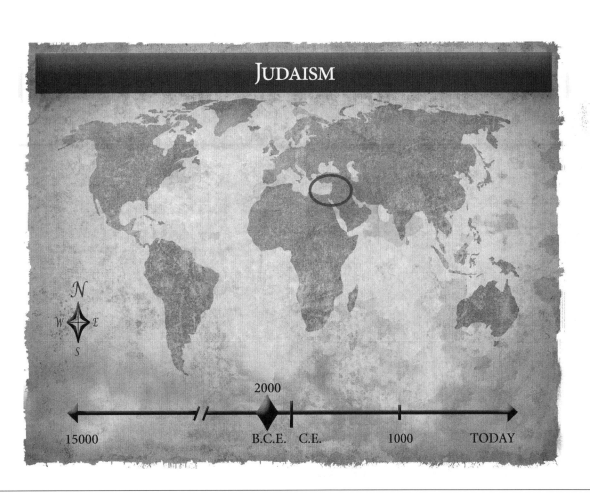

JUDAISM

5. Hinduism

"This is the sum of duty: do not do to others what would cause pain if done to you."
—*Mahabharata 5:1517*

"This is the sum of all true righteousness: treat others as thou wouldst thyself be treated. Do nothing to thy neighbor which hereafter thou wouldst not have thy neighbor do to thee."
—*Mahabharata (Ganguli, Book 13, CXIII)*

HINDUISM is a complex mosaic of religious beliefs that defies simple definition and explanation. This complexity reflects the vast diversity of the Indian subcontinent, where Hinduism was born.

One belief that is widely accepted in Hinduism is **reincarnation.** To Hindus, the body is only a temporary vessel for an eternal soul. When the body dies, the soul's journey in the temporal world is not over. Instead, the soul, the eternal spiritual essence that had inhabited the body, will be merged with another body and "reborn" into the material world. A soul's karma, the sum total of the soul's good and bad actions, determines the quality of life that the soul will be born into. The cycle of death and rebirth continues until the soul has reached perfection, at which time it is liberated and merges with the divine.

---

reincarnation: the rebirth of a soul in a new body

① Explain karma in your own words.

_____

_____

_____

_____

_____

② How do you think the concept of _reincarnation_ relates to the Golden Rule in Hinduism?

_____

_____

_____

_____

_____

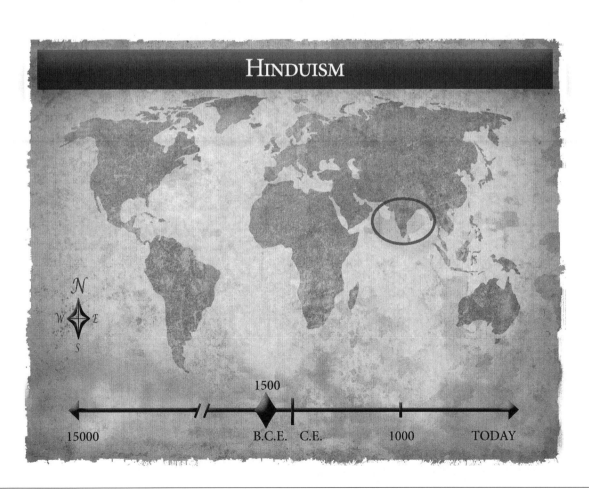

HINDUISM

1500

15000   B.C.E.   C.E.   1000   TODAY

6. ZOROASTRIANISM

"That nature alone is good which refrains from doing unto another whatsoever is not good for itself."
—Dadistan-i-dinik 94:5

"Whatever is disagreeable to yourself do not do unto others."
—Shayast-na-Shayast 13:29

ZOROASTRIANISM sees the universe as a battleground in an epic struggle between good and evil, a view known as **dualism.** Zoroastrians worship Ahura Mazda, an entirely good and benevolent god who created the universe and is the ultimate source of all good in it. Pitted against Ahura Mazda and the forces of good is Angra Mainyu, a destructive being who is the root of all evil.

Zoroastrians believe human beings have an important role to play in the struggle between good and evil. Humans must reject evil, both in their own lives and in the world around them, and be active agents for promoting good. This can be accomplished in part by adhering to the Golden Rule. When Ahura Mazda triumphs over Angra Mainyu and good has defeated evil, human souls will rejoin Ahura Mazda in the spiritual realm for an eternity of peace.

---

dualism: the religious doctrine that the universe contains opposed powers of good and evil

① How might differing perspectives on good and evil affect how people observe the Golden Rule?

_____

_____

_____

_____

_____

② Review the second version of the Golden Rule, which begins "Whatever is disagreeable…." Compare it to the Christian "Do to others what you would have them do to you, for this sums up the Law and the Prophets."

_____

_____

_____

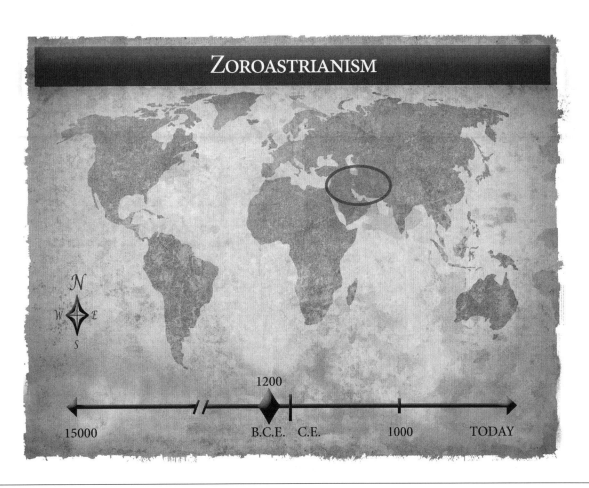

ZOROASTRIANISM

1200

15000   B.C.E.   C.E.   1000   TODAY

7. Confucianism

"Do not do to others what you do not want them to do to you."
—Analects 15:23

"Tzu Kung asked: 'Is there any one principle upon which one's whole life may proceed?' Confucius replied: 'Is not Reciprocity such a principle? Do not impose on others what you yourself do not desire.'"
—Doctrine of the Mean 13.3

"Try your best to treat others as you would wish to be treated yourself, and you will find that this is the shortest way to benevolence."
—Mencius VII.A.4

CONFUCIANISM is based largely on the teachings of Confucius, a Chinese scholar and social philosopher. It focuses on hierarchical relationships, respect, and social order. It defines the roles of people in society based upon their relationship to others, and outlines important human virtues such as loyalty, sincerity, and justice.

The **founder** of a religion can play a large or defining role. In the case of Confucianism, the founder's teachings and wisdom were not only central to the development of the religion, but also became its exact tenets. Still today, the ideas of Confucius are widely respected and continue to have an impact on Chinese society.

---

founder: originator or creator of a religion

① Confucianism emphasizes hierarchical relationships. Do you think this is in keeping with the Golden Rule? Explain.

_____

_____

_____

_____

_____

② Do you agree with the idea that "Reciprocity" is a "principle upon which one's whole life may proceed"? Why or why not?

_____

_____

_____

_____

_____

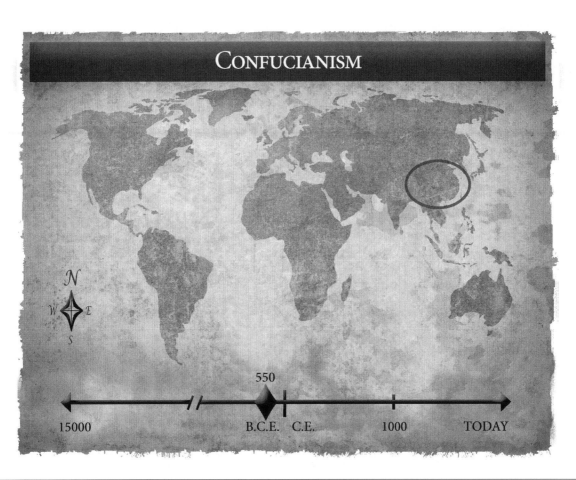

8. JAINISM

*"Therefore, neither does he [a sage] cause violence to others
nor does he make others do so."*
—Acarangasutra 5.101-2

*"In happiness and suffering, in joy and grief, we should regard all creatures
as we regard our own self."*
—Lord Mahavira, 24th Tirthankar

"A man should wander about treating all creatures as he himself would be treated."
—Sutrakritanga Sutra 1.11.33

JAINISM calls for its followers to pursue a lifestyle of **asceticism,** the practice of rigid self-discipline and abstention from all forms of indulgence. Of course, not all Jains strictly adhere to such a lifestyle, but some divergence between belief and practice is a feature of all religions.

Jains are expected to do no harm to any living thing (and therefore must be vegetarian), to possess only what they absolutely need, and use all extra possessions to benefit other people in the community. They must not lie, including by omission. In every realm of life they are expected to live simply and use the fewest resources possible. Jain monks and nuns live by an even stricter ascetic code; monks of one sect reject all material possessions, including clothes. The rationale behind living an ascetic life is that it frees the soul and the mind from temporal concerns so that one can focus wholly on spiritual growth.

---

asceticism: the practice of strict self-discipline and self-denial,
usually for religious or spiritual reasons

① Can observing the Golden Rule eliminate all harm, as Jains attempt to do? Why or why not?

_____

_____

_____

② What do you think "lie by omission" means?

_____

_____

_____

③ How does Jainism's versions of the Golden Rule differ from most other religions' versions? (Hint: consider the choice of the word "creatures.")

_____

_____

_____

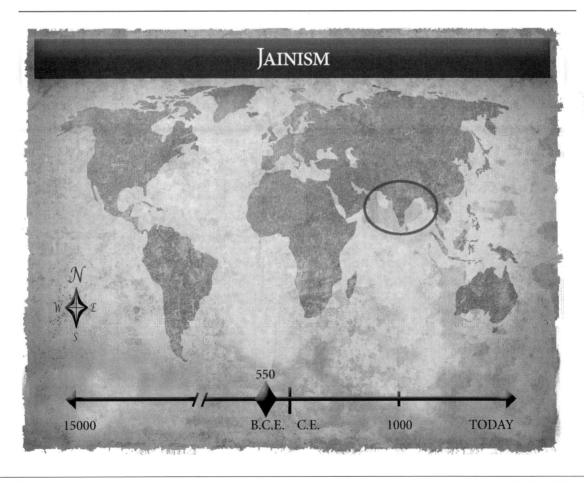

JAINISM

550

15000   B.C.E.   C.E.   1000   TODAY

9. Buddhism

"Hurt not others in ways that you yourself would find hurtful."
—Udana-Varga 5:18

*" ...a state that is not pleasing or delightful to me,
how could I inflict that upon another?"*
—Samyutta Nikaya v. 353

Unlike most religions, Buddhism's focus is not the worship of a deity. In fact, Buddhism lacks anything that could be described as a deity, leading scholars to refer to it as an example of **nontheism.** Instead of worshipping a god, Buddhists devote themselves to personal spiritual development. They seek spiritual growth and ultimately Enlightenment through meditation, prayer, chanting, venerating the Buddha, seeking wisdom, and introspection.

There are many Buddhist temples all over the world, but it is not considered necessary for a Buddhist to worship at a temple. This is rooted in the central philosophy of Buddhism, which treats spiritual growth as a personal matter and states that each person must find his or her own path to Enlightenment.

---

nontheism: the absence of belief in a deity

① How might *nontheism* influence a person's view of the world?

_____

_____

_____

_____

_____

② Why might the Golden Rule be especially important in a nontheist religion?

_____

_____

_____

_____

_____

_____

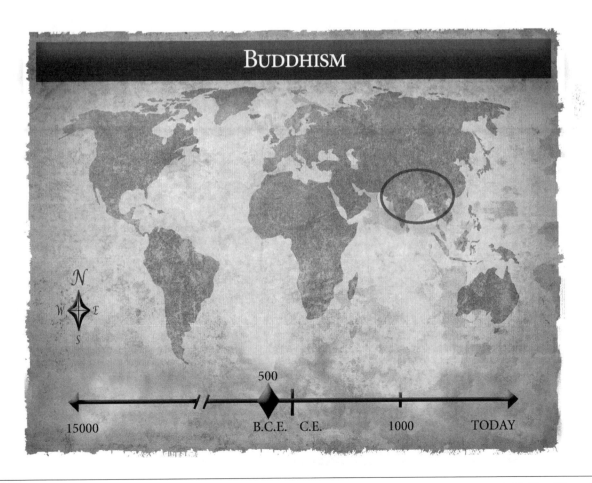

10. ROMAN PAGAN RELIGION

*"The law imprinted on the hearts of all men
is to love the members of society as themselves."*
—Roman saying

THE ROMAN PAGAN RELIGION was a thoroughly **polytheistic** faith, as worship was directed towards numerous gods and goddesses. Each deity had his or her own realm, such as Neptune, god of the sea, and Apollo, god of the sun. Unlike the deities of many religions, Roman gods and goddesses were neither supremely good nor all-powerful. Instead, they exhibited human traits such as lust and jealousy, procreated with other deities as well as with humans, and had power only over their own realms.

The gods were thought to regularly intervene in human affairs, so Romans sought the favor and protection of the gods through worship, sacrifice, and offerings. Temples for all the various deities were erected throughout the Roman world, and some were extraordinarily lavish. In many ways, the polytheism of the Roman religion was central to Roman life.

---

polytheism: the belief in or worship of more than one god

① The gods in the Roman Pagan Religion do not always adhere to the Golden Rule. What, then, might motivate Roman believers in the gods to do so? Should the followers still try to?

_____

_____

_____

_____

② The human traits of the gods distinguished them from the perfectly just, and all-loving deities of monotheistic religions around the same time. Compare and contrast the desirable facets of a perfect god with the desirable facets of an imperfect god.

_____

_____

_____

_____

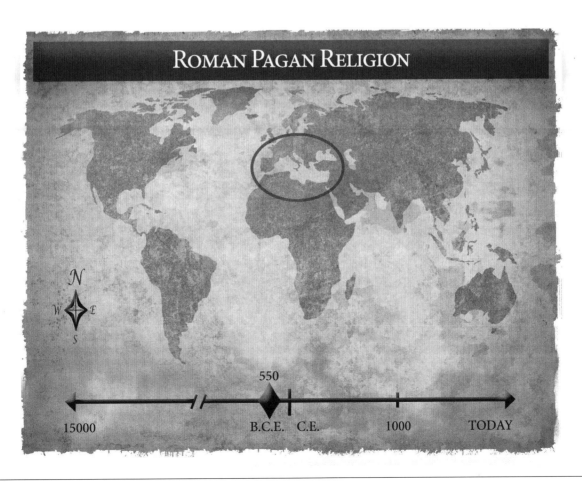

11. TAOISM

"Regard you neighbor's gain as your own gain; and regard your neighbor's loss as your own loss, even as though you were in their place."
—Tai-Shan Kan-Ying P'ien (Treatise on Action and Recompense)

"The sage has no interest of his own, but takes the interests of the people as his own. He is kind to the kind; he is also kind to the unkind: for Virtue is kind. He is faithful to the faithful; he is also faithful to the unfaithful: for Virtue is faithful."
—Tao Te Ching, Chapter 49

TAOISM is concerned with order and harmony at cosmic, social, and individual levels. The goal of Taoist practices is to bring about and maintain order and harmony, and ultimately to attain unity with the universe and spiritual immortality. The Golden Rule in Taoism is rooted in these concepts and is a means to seek harmony in human society.

As in many Eastern religions, **meditation** is an important Taoist practice. Meditation is a mental exercise involving quiet contemplation and the focusing of one's thoughts. It can bring about a trance-like state that is thought to enhance spiritual understanding. In a Taoist context, meditation is a tool used to seek inner order and harmony and to seek an understanding of the world around us towards the goal of achieving unity with the universe.

---

meditation: engaging in mental exercises for the purpose of reaching a heightened level of spiritual awareness

① Balance and harmony are concepts mentioned in many religions. Do you think these are important in human life? Why or why not?

_____

_____

_____

_____

_____

② Explain what you think the Golden Rule's role in achieving Taoist goals of harmony is.

_____

_____

_____

_____

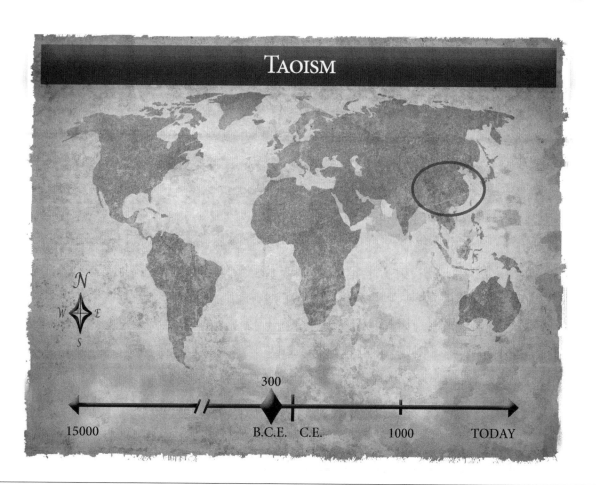

12. CHRISTIANITY

"And as ye would that men should do to you, do ye also to them likewise."
—*Luke 6:31, King James Version*

*"So in everything, do to others what you would have them do to you,
for this sums up the Law and the Prophets."*
—*Matthew 7:12, NIV*

At the heart of Christianity is a **doctrine of salvation.** In Christianity, all human souls have an eternal fate: either total bliss in Heaven, or perpetual torment in Hell. Christians believe that in order to enter Heaven, humans must be delivered from sin.

The Christian doctrine of salvation centers on Jesus of Nazareth. Christians believe that Jesus was Christ the Messiah, the Son of God sent to earth to redeem humanity. Jesus took on the sins of man and paid the price for them through his suffering and crucifixion. So, in the Christian belief system, having faith in Jesus as the Son of God and following his teachings is the path to redemption from sin. Thus, it is also the path to God and eternal life in Heaven.

Jesus himself is the source of the Golden Rule in Christianity, and thus it is a fundamental Christian concept. Christians believe the life of Jesus was entirely free from sin, so it offers an example of a perfect human life. Observing the Golden Rule is a way for Christians to steer clear of sin.

---

doctrine of salvation: a set of beliefs concerning deliverance
from sin and its consequences

① Explain the role of a *doctrine of salvation* in religion.

_____

_____

_____

② Why is the Golden Rule so foundational in Christianity?

_____

_____

_____

③ The Christian version of the Golden Rule is arguably the best known worldwide.
Why might this be so?

_____

_____

_____

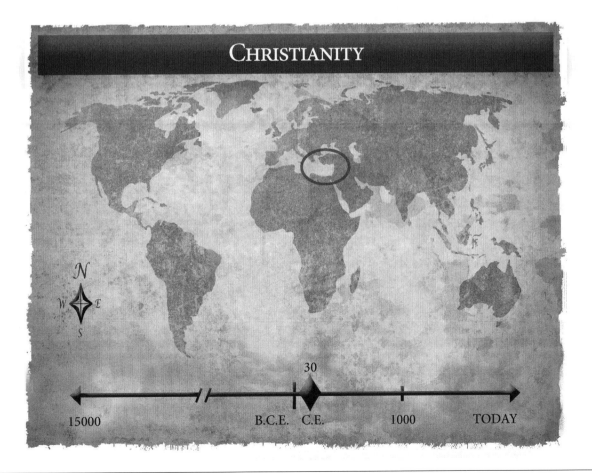

13. Shinto

"The heart of the person before you is a mirror. See there your own form."
—Shinto proverb

"Be charitable to all beings, love is the representative of God."
—Ko-ji-ki Hachiman Kasuga

SHINTO is the traditional religion of Japan. Shintoists believe in *kami*, which means, "that which is hidden." In English, *kami* is often translated as "spirits." Generally, *kami* are regarded as the mystical or sacred element of anything in existence. They are beings, more powerful than humans but not gods, and they give meaning to things, be it a waterfall, an animal, a landscape, or a force of nature. They inhabit this world and are present among humans, as opposed to existing in an unreachable spiritual realm.

Shinto believers worship kami (different ones depending on the situation) through **rituals,** ceremonies that follow established forms. Many Shinto rituals are elaborate and exhibit great attention to aesthetics. Shinto shrines and temples are the site of the most important and formal rituals, and simpler rituals such as offerings and prayers take place at home.

---

ritual: a solemn or religious ceremony consisting of a series of actions performed according to a prescribed order

① How does the presence of sacred *kami* in the human world and not in another realm make Shinto different from other major religions?

_____

_____

_____

_____

_____

② What do you think is the role or roles of *rituals* in religion?

_____

_____

_____

_____

_____

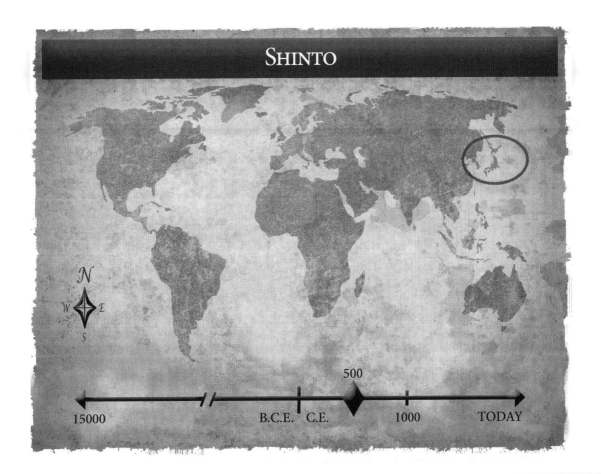

14. ISLAM

"None of you [truly] believes until he wishes for his brother
what he wishes for himself."
—*Saying of the Prophet Muhammad,*
in Imam Al-Nawawi's Forty Hadiths, Number 13

"Do unto all men as you would they should do unto you,
and reject for others what you would reject for yourself."
—*Saying of the Prophet Muhammad, in Mishkat Al-Masabih*

The Islamic concept of the Golden Rule is laid out in the *hadiths,* which are recorded sayings and deeds of the Prophet Muhammad.

The concern for other people that is central to the Golden Rule is reinforced in Islam by a charitable tax called the *zakah,* one of the Five Pillars of Faith, the most important Muslim religious obligations.

The first of the Five Pillars is the central tenet of Islam, the Profession of Faith: "There is no god but God, and Muhammad is His messenger." This statement expresses belief in **monotheism,** the doctrine that there is only one true God. Violating the monotheistic principle of belief is *shirk,* the gravest sin a Muslim can commit.

Islam is linked with two older monotheistic faiths, Christianity and Judaism, which are parts of the same religious tradition. Together the three are called the Abrahamic faiths, because of their shared belief in Abraham as an important prophet of God. Muslims believe Jews and Christians worship the same God that they do.

---

monotheism: the doctrine or belief that there is only one true God

① What might belief in a *monotheistic* religion reflect about a society, if anything?

_____

_____

_____

_____

_____

② What role do prophets play in the development of religion?

_____

_____

_____

_____

_____

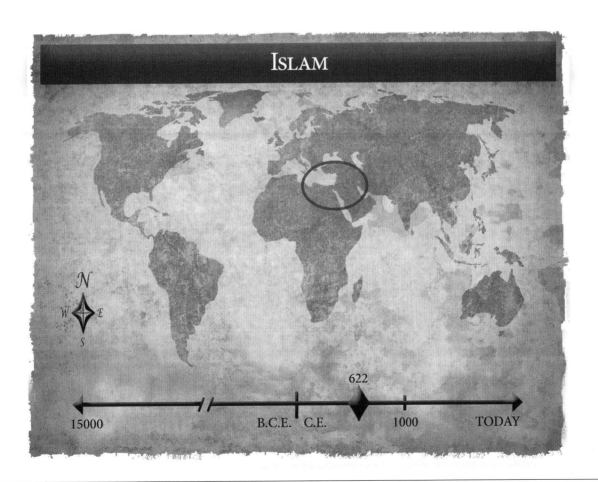

ISLAM

622

15000   B.C.E. C.E.   1000   TODAY

15. SUFISM

"The basis of Sufism is consideration of the hearts and feelings of others. If you haven't the will to gladden someone's heart, then at least beware lest you hurt someone's heart, for on our path, no sin exists but this."
—*Dr. Javad Nurbakhsh, Master of the Nimatullahi Sufi Order*

SUFISM is most often described as Islamic **mysticism.** Mysticism is a path of devotion that stresses that spiritual growth, insight into ultimate reality, and knowledge of God can be attained through personal experiences. Many religions have traditions of mysticism within them, including all three Abrahamic faiths.

Sufis are practicing Muslims, usually highly devout ones, and are set apart only by their choice to follow the path of mysticism. Their ultimate goal is total devotion to God in all aspects of life. They seek knowledge of and personal communion with God, through a variety of means. Common practices are meditation on the Quran, fasting, rejection of worldly comforts, chanting, singing, and dance.

---

mysticism: the belief that direct knowledge of God, spiritual truth, or ultimate reality can be attained through subjective experience (as intuition or insight)

1. Explain *mysticism* in your own words.

_____

_____

_____

_____

2. Why do you think the practice of mysticism is found within so many religions?

_____

_____

_____

_____

_____

_____

_____

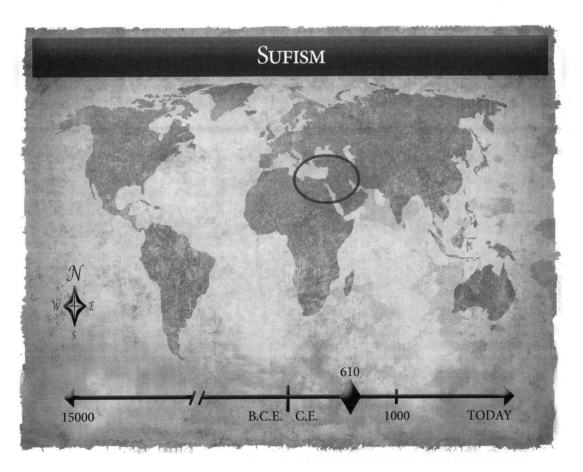

SUFISM

610

15000   B.C.E.   C.E.   1000   TODAY

16. SIKHISM

"Don't create enmity with anyone as God is within everyone."
—Guru Arjan Devji, 259

"No one is my enemy, none a stranger and everyone is my friend."
—Guru Arjan Devji, AG 1299

"Treat others as thou wouldst be treated thyself."
—Guru Angad, Macauliffe v. 2

SIKHISM is a monotheistic faith that stresses honesty, hard work, good actions, equality, and generosity. These central beliefs underpin the Sikh conception of the Golden Rule.

Sikhs place great importance on their **scripture,** or holy book, the Guru Granth Sahib. It is regarded as an ever-present teacher and treated with deep reverence and respect. It sits on a cushion atop a platform and under a canopy, and when not in use is often covered with an ornate cloth. Interestingly, it includes teachings, poems, and hymns from not only Sikh Gurus, but also Hindus and Muslims. At every Sikh ceremony, a copy of the Guru Granth Sahib is present.

At the Golden Temple, Sikhism's holiest place, the Guru Granth Sahib is read continuously, around the clock and throughout the year. To mark important events, such as a wedding, birth, or Sikh holy day, a cover-to-cover reading of the Guru Granth Sahib is held. A number of readers take turns, and the process lasts about 48 hours. This reading, called an akhand paath, is considered one of the holiest Sikh ceremonies.

---

scripture: a body of writings considered sacred or authoritative

① What is the importance of *scripture* to a religion?

_____

_____

_____

② Does the fact that some religions lack a scripture cause them to function differently? Why or why not?

_____

_____

_____

③ Which of the three quotations do you like best? Why?

_____

_____

_____

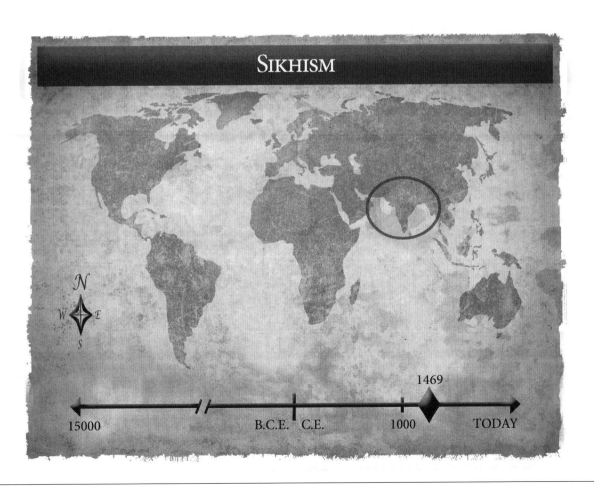

SIKHISM

17. HUMANISM

"Humanists acknowledge human interdependence, the need for mutual respect and the kinship of all humanity.... Humanists affirm that individual and social problems can only be resolved by means of human reason, intelligent effort, critical thinking joined with compassion and a spirit of empathy for all living beings."
—British Humanist Society

"Critical intelligence, infused by a sense of human caring, is the best method that humanity has for resolving problems. Reason should be balanced with compassion and empathy and the whole person fulfilled."
—Humanist Manifesto II, Ethics section

HUMANISM is a philosophy that espouses the importance of human reason coupled with empathy and compassion. It stands alone as a **secular** philosophy, but has also had profound influence on many religions. Today there are humanist strains of Christianity, Judaism, Islam, and many others of the world's faiths.

Many humanists are atheists who do not believe that a god exists. They point to such things as the evolutionary advantages of reciprocity and kindness as natural sources for human morality.

The impact of humanism serves as an example of how religions can change over time through interpretation. Religious humanists stress different aspects of religion than the orthodox interpretations. They see human reason as a gift from God, and put faith in the power of reason as a means to solve the world's problems, large and small.

---

secular: denoting attitudes, activities, or other things
that have no religious or spiritual basis

① How might the expression of a *secular* Golden Rule inform your understanding of the idea behind it?

_____

_____

_____

_____

_____

② In your opinion, why is the Golden Rule found in so many religions around the world and throughout history?

_____

_____

_____

_____

_____

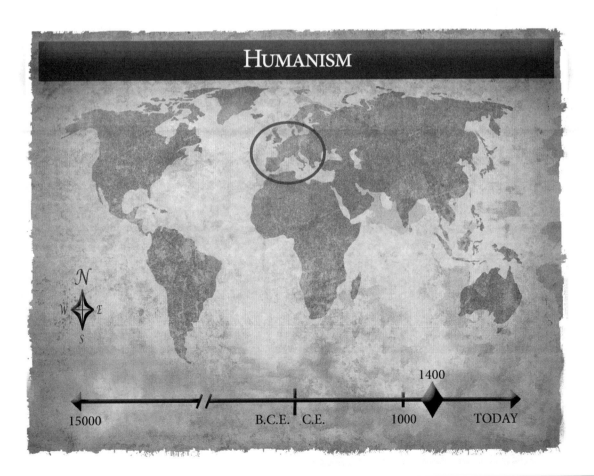

18. Baha'i

"Blessed is he who preferreth his brother before himself."
—Baha'u'llah

"And if thine eyes be turned towards justice, choose thou for thy neighbor that which thou choosest for thyself."
—Epistle to the Son of the Wolf

"Ascribe not to any soul that which thou wouldst not have ascribed to thee, and say not that which thou doest not."
—Baha'u'llah, The Hidden Words of Baha'u'llah, 29

The Baha'i religion is based primarily on the teachings of Baha'u'allah, whom Baha'is believe was a prophet of God. The fundamental message of Baha'i is the unity of all mankind and of all religions. Baha'is believe that all of the world's major religions legitimately came from God, and in fact are not different religions but just separate stages of the same religion. The fundamental messages of religions are seen not only as compatible, but identical. This blending of religious traditions is called **syncretism.**

To Baha'is, the Golden Rule is humanity's most important moral imperative, as well as a perfect example of the oneness of all religions. Baha'is see the Golden Rule as essential to the unity of mankind, the elimination of prejudice, and the effort towards world peace.

---

syncretism: the combination of different beliefs or practices; the amalgamation of different religions

① Explain *syncretism* and how Baha'i exhibits this process.

_____

_____

_____

② Keeping in mind the Baha'i belief that the Golden Rule is essential for world peace, evaluate this statement: "The Golden Rule cannot effectively be applied in all situations when there are others who will not abide by it."

_____

_____

_____

_____

_____

_____

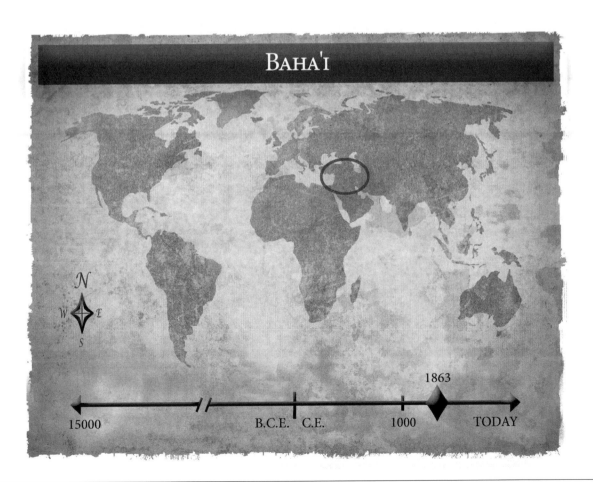

19. WICCA

"If it harms no one, do what thou wilt."
—The Wiccan Rede

*"All good that a person does to another returns threefold in this life;
harm is also returned threefold."*
—The Threefold Law

WICCA is a modern system of belief that is part of a larger religious movement that incorporates ancient pagan beliefs. As such, it falls under the umbrella of **neopaganism.** Neopaganism is a loosely defined movement that generally stresses recognition of and connection to natural cycles. Neopagan rituals and festivals usually revolve around days of natural significance, such as the solstices and equinoxes.

Wiccans believe supernatural forces can be harnessed and directed through rituals and incantations, but are prohibited from harming others with supernatural power by the Wiccan Rede. The Rede, quoted above, serves as the central guiding principle in Wiccan life. Wiccans value total freedom of thought, expression, and action, and the Rede is the sole limiting factor to that freedom.

---

neopaganism: a modern religious movement that seeks to incorporate beliefs or ritual practices from traditions from outside the main world religions, especially pre-Christian Europe and North America

① Do you think the Wiccan Rede is equivalent to the Golden Rule? Why or why not?

_____

_____

_____

② Why do you think so many religions focus on natural cycles in one way or another?

_____

_____

_____

③ Religious movements are often a response to societal stresses. What pressures do you think might have spawned the modern _neopaganist_ movement?

_____

_____

_____

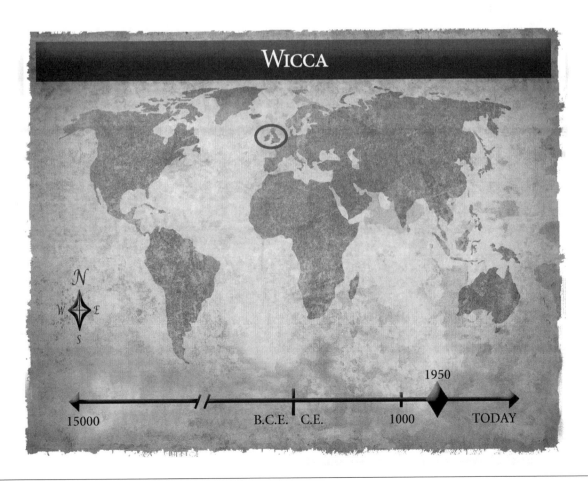

20. UNITARIAN UNIVERSALISM

"Unitarian Universalist congregations affirm and promote: The inherent worth and dignity of every person; justice, equity and compassion in human relations... the goal of world community with peace, liberty, and justice for all; and respect for the interdependent web of all existence of which we are a part."
—*Unitarian Universalist Principles, 1, 2, 6, 7*

UNITARIAN UNIVERSALISM is often described as a **non-creedal** religion, meaning there is no one doctrine that members are expected to adhere to. Most religions mandate a set of beliefs, such as faith in only one god, in a sacred text, or in a specific doctrine of salvation. Unitarian Universalism, on the other hand, is open to people of all beliefs. Some congregation members believe in many gods, some believe in one, and some have no belief in any.

The common denominator among Unitarian Universalists is the search for truth, meaning, and personal spiritual growth. Unitarian Universalists think that an authoritative religious body (i.e. a religion with a mandated creed) hinders this search and, thus, limits a person's theological perspective. The Seven Principles, four of which are given above, are meant to guide members in their search.

---

non-creedal: the property of lacking a set of beliefs

① Explain the role of a *creed* in religion.

_____

_____

_____

_____

_____

② In your opinion, can the Golden Rule function as a universal ethic? Is it, as the name suggests, the ultimate measure of whether one is behaving ethically? Explain your reasoning.

_____

_____

_____

_____

_____

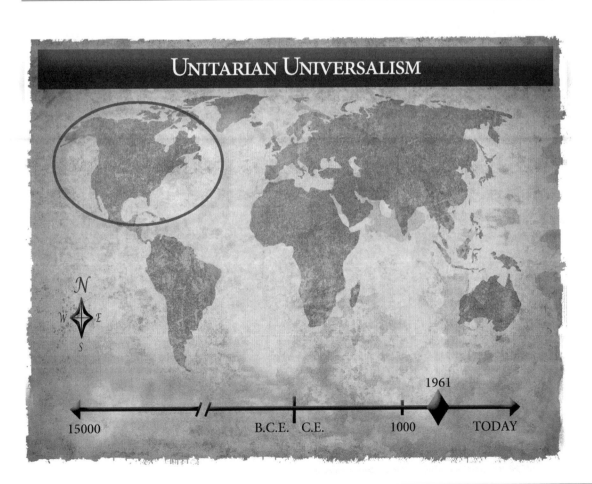

UNITARIAN UNIVERSALISM

21. Following the Golden Rule

Reflect on what you have learned about the Golden Rule.
Answer the questions.

① Which expression of the Golden Rule do you find most appealing? Why?

_____

_____

_____

② Do you think the Golden Rule alone provides individuals with enough guidance to lead "good" lives? Explain your answer.

_____

_____

_____

③ Write about a time when you or someone you know did or did not follow the Golden Rule. What were the consequences?

_____

_____

_____

_____

_____

④ What does the Golden Rule mean to you?

_____

_____

_____

_____

_____

_____

_____

_____

_____

_____

⑤ Circle the continents where the Golden Rule has been advocated. Use the time line to indicate when the Golden Rule has been advocated.

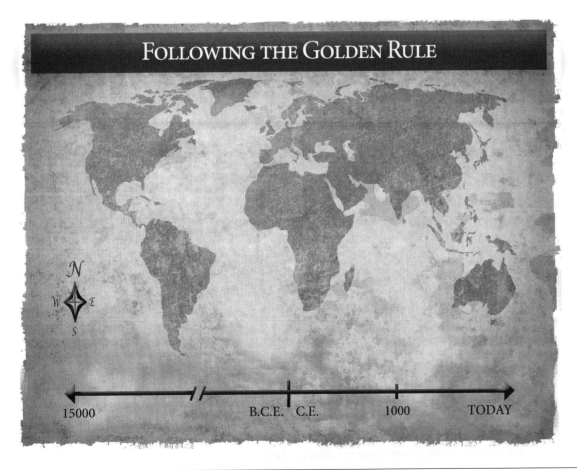

FOLLOWING THE GOLDEN RULE

Printed in Great Britain
by Amazon

28609634R00031